AF688186

Voice AI Agents

Build Phone Bots, Voice Assistants & AI Receptionists Without Code

By Joe Correa

Published by Live Stronger Faster

This book is for educational and informational purposes only. The author and publisher are not engaged in rendering legal, financial, or other professional advice. Readers should consult a qualified professional before making any financial decisions.

First Edition

Table of Contents

Introduction

Voice is becoming the new interface of the digital world. After decades of typing, clicking, tapping, scrolling, and navigating menus, we are entering an era where people can interact with technology the way human beings have interacted with each other since the beginning of time—through natural speech. Voice assistants, AI receptionists, phone-answering bots, automated booking systems, conversational agents, and real-time voice responders are no longer futuristic luxuries reserved for billion-dollar companies. With today's no-code tools like Voiceflow, ElevenLabs, Speak.ai, Aircall, Twilio, and GPT-powered conversational engines, literally anyone—including complete beginners—can build professional-grade voice AI agents that handle calls, route customers, book appointments, gather information, deliver instructions, answer questions, and automate tasks twenty-four hours a day without ever picking up the phone. This book will show you how to do exactly that. It will take you step by step through the exact frameworks, decisions, tools, architectures, conversations, flows, and voice design methods used by the world's top AI builders—except you won't need to write even a single line of code.

Voice AI is unique because it blends technology with psychology. It requires an understanding of how people speak, how conversations unfold, what users expect in the first three seconds of a phone call, and what makes a voice sound trustworthy, friendly, human, helpful, or authoritative. A voice agent has to understand interruptions, handle mistakes, clarify questions, confirm details, react quickly, and remain calm regardless of how chaotic the caller may be. Unlike text chatbots, voice agents must manage tone, timing, pacing, intonation, silence, and natural rhythms. When done correctly, the results are powerful. Voice AI can feel more human than live customer support teams. It never gets tired, never gets frustrated, never experiments with inconsistent answers, and never forgets a single instruction. And because these systems can be duplicated infinitely, your business can scale faster than ever before with no extra staff, no extra office, and no extra payroll. You will learn how to design voice interactions that feel natural, safe, effective, and genuinely enjoyable.

One of the biggest misconceptions about AI voice agents is the belief that they require complex engineering, programming, and expensive phone infrastructure. That used to be true... but not anymore. Today's voice platforms offer simple drag-and-drop builders, ready-to-use modules, natural language understanding powered by GPT, and voice synthesis so realistic that most callers cannot distinguish them from humans. You can create custom voices, clone your own voice, generate accents, adjust tone, and script dynamic responses that change based on caller intent, account data, time of day, or whatever rules you choose. You can integrate your voice agent with CRMs, scheduling tools, databases, Google Sheets, help desks, email systems, and even full AI workflows that take action automatically. The power available to everyday creators today is the equivalent of having your own private voice-enabled call center with infinite employees, perfect memory, and perfect reliability—all for a small monthly subscription.

This book will guide you through real-world use cases across multiple industries so you can build voice agents with purpose, clarity, and professional quality. You will build intake agents for real estate and mortgage businesses. You will build appointment-booking assistants for service providers. You will build AI receptionists for small businesses that want professional call coverage without hiring staff. You will build customer support agents that answer FAQs, troubleshoot steps, collect details, and escalate when necessary. You will build sales agents that guide callers through qualifying steps and hand off high-quality leads to the right person. You will build voice assistants for personal productivity, daily reminders, personal research, and even AI self-coaching. By the end of this book, you will not simply know *how* voice AI works—you will know how to deploy it across any industry, goal, or personal project.

As you progress, you'll learn the psychology of voice agent design. You'll understand the importance of the first four seconds, where callers decide instantly whether they trust the agent. You'll learn how to design prompts that feel conversational rather than robotic. You'll learn how to handle ambiguity, interruptions, confusion, and incomplete answers. You'll discover how to implement decision trees, dynamic routing, fallback paths, sentiment detection, and advanced logic. You will learn the secrets of building voice agents that adapt, learn, and improve over time. By the end of the first few chapters, you'll already have a working prototype. By the time you reach the final chapter, you'll be building full multi-step, multi-tool, revenue-generating systems that rival major companies. And you will have done it all without writing code.

What makes voice AI especially powerful in today's world is the rise of realistic synthetic speech. ElevenLabs, in particular, has transformed what is possible. You can build voices that sound warm, friendly, confident, or professional. You can generate multilingual agents that speak English, Spanish, Portuguese, French, German, and more—allowing global coverage from day one. You can produce agents that personalize their tone based on the caller: more energetic for new leads, more relaxed for customer support, more authoritative for security or verification flows. The ability to custom-design voices unlocks branding opportunities that have never existed before. Your business can literally have its own signature voice—an instantly recognizable AI representative that becomes part of your identity.

The purpose of this book is simple: to give you the knowledge, the frameworks, the tools, the templates, and the practical skills needed to build professional, automated, scalable voice AI systems that save you time, generate revenue, support customers, and elevate your brand. Whether you are a business owner, a freelancer, a marketer, a creator, a customer support manager, or someone exploring new AI opportunities, this book will equip you with everything you need to build voice AI agents that feel human, deliver value, and operate automatically around the clock. You will walk away with a toolkit that can be applied to any idea or industry, and the confidence to build voice experiences that transform how people interact with your business.

Chapter 1

Understanding the Power of Voice AI Agents

Voice AI is quickly becoming one of the most valuable technologies in the new era of automation because it brings the most natural human interface—speech—into the digital world. Before voice AI, customer communication depended on slow text chats, endless email back-and-forth, or expensive call centers that required hiring, training, supervising, and constantly managing people. But now, with GPT-powered speech recognition and ultra-realistic synthetic voices, you can build voice agents that talk, listen, respond, clarify, and take action the same way a trained employee would. These agents can answer calls around the clock without missing a single detail, providing next-level customer service without ever needing a salary, breaks, or sleep. Understanding the power behind voice AI is the foundation of everything you will build in this book and the key to unlocking an entirely new level of efficiency for your business.

Voice AI agents differ from chatbots because voice is not just another interface—it is a completely different cognitive experience for the user. When someone speaks, they expect instant acknowledgment, natural rhythm, conversational pacing, and smooth back-and-forth flow. Designing for voice requires you to understand not only the technology behind the agent but also how humans naturally communicate when they're stressed, confused, busy, distracted, or in a hurry. Voice interactions depend heavily on tone, timing, emotion, and clarity. A well-designed agent can guide a caller through complex steps, gather details, provide answers, and route them to the right outcome without ever feeling robotic or scripted. This ability to create a deeply human experience is what separates powerful voice AI agents from basic automated phone systems of the past.

Modern voice technology is powered by several blended forces: natural language understanding (NLU), text-to-speech (TTS), speech-to-text (STT), decision logic, and AI-driven context memory. When a caller speaks, the speech-to-text engine immediately converts their voice into written words. The large language model interprets what was said, extracts intent, identifies relevant information, and chooses the appropriate response. Then, text-to-speech transforms that response back into spoken words using a customized AI voice. All of this happens in fractions of a second, creating the illusion of natural, fluid conversation. The result is a system that feels alive—one that responds to questions, listens actively, and adapts in real time. This is why companies worldwide are replacing human receptionists, appointment schedulers, support teams, and phone agents with AI-powered voice systems.

Because voice AI is capable of handling more than simple question-and-answer exchanges, you can integrate advanced automation into every conversation. Your agent can check calendars, book appointments, fill out forms, send reminders, create CRM entries, trigger Make.com workflows, update Google Sheets, submit tickets, check order statuses, qualify leads, or escalate calls to a human. With the right setup, your voice agent becomes an intelligent operations assistant that does the job of multiple people simultaneously. Understanding this potential helps you design systems that can run entire departments on autopilot while giving your customers immediate and consistent experiences every time they call.

Voiceflow, ElevenLabs, Twilio, and similar tools allow you to build these experiences without code and without having to understand the underlying complexity of speech technology. Voiceflow provides the visual interface for creating the call flow—what your agent says, what it listens for, and what actions it takes. ElevenLabs gives you natural-sounding voices that you can customize to fit your brand's personality. Twilio and Aircall give your agent a phone number, call routing, and telephony infrastructure. Make.com and Zapier allow you to automate the tasks triggered by each call. When you combine these tools, you gain the ability to design voice agents that sound human, think intelligently, and take action automatically—all without programming. The no-code revolution has made it possible for beginners, business owners, and creators to build advanced voice systems in a single afternoon.

As you progress through this book, your understanding of voice AI will evolve from basic concepts to advanced agent design. You will learn how to create conversation flows, handle interruptions, design prompts that feel natural, choose the right voice personality, capture accurate caller data, and integrate tools that automate tasks behind the scenes. You will build agents that sell, support, qualify, direct, or guide users based on their needs. You will understand how to structure conversations so your agent never gets stuck, confused, or repetitive. Most importantly, you will gain confidence in building systems that replace repetitive manual work and elevate your customer experience to a level most businesses cannot match. Before you begin building your first agent, you must fully understand the power and potential you now have access to. That foundation is exactly what this first chapter gives you.

"The Assistant Who Never Slept"

The phones never stopped ringing at Clara's small real estate office. Every morning, from the moment she unlocked the front door, the blinking red lights of missed calls reminded her of the same problem she had battled for years: there were simply too many callers and not enough staff. Some people wanted to see a property. Others wanted to schedule a loan consultation. Others needed to verify paperwork or ask questions about a listing. Clara had built her business from nothing, but she was drowning in calls. Every unanswered phone call felt like a missed opportunity, and every frustrated caller felt like a failure weighing on her shoulders. She tried hiring assistants, but they came and went, leaving behind inconsistent service and stress. She knew something had to change.

One night, overwhelmed and exhausted, Clara stumbled across an article about AI voice agents. It described systems that could answer calls, talk to customers, gather details, schedule appointments, and even speak multiple languages. At first, she dismissed it as something only big companies could use—something expensive and complicated, far beyond her reach. But curiosity kept pulling her back. She discovered Voiceflow, ElevenLabs, and Twilio. She watched a demonstration of an AI receptionist who greeted callers naturally, asked questions, understood emotions, and routed calls to the right person. Clara felt something she hadn't felt in months: hope.

She decided to try building her own voice AI agent. She named it "Sophie." At first, Sophie sounded robotic, asking questions with the flat, emotionless tone of a machine. But as Clara refined the script, adjusted the prompts, and experimented with a warmer ElevenLabs voice, Sophie began to sound like a real human assistant—kind, patient, consistent. Clara trained Sophie to ask for caller names, collect details, check the office calendar, schedule appointments, and send confirmations. She taught Sophie how to calm anxious callers and guide first-time buyers with reassuring clarity. When Clara connected Sophie to her CRM through Make.com, the agent became fully functional, instantly recording lead information and updating the system automatically.

The first day Sophie went live, Clara held her breath. She watched the call dashboard as Sophie answered call after call, greeting each person with polished professionalism. She handled scheduling. She gathered details. She even switched gracefully between English and Spanish depending on what the caller spoke. For the first time in years, Clara didn't feel the panic of juggling conversations. She didn't feel the guilt of missing calls. She didn't feel the overwhelm of constant interruptions. Instead, she felt free. She could focus on clients, listings, paperwork, and strategy—without being chained to the phone.

Within a week, Sophie had handled over two hundred calls flawlessly. Clara's clients praised "the new assistant" who never seemed rushed and always sounded cheerful. Several callers even asked if Sophie could help them with things outside regular office hours. They were shocked to discover she was available at 2 AM. They were even more shocked when they learned she wasn't human at all. Every day, Clara looked at the call logs in disbelief. The agent had not missed a single call. Not one. For the first time in her business, consistency was no longer a dream—it was a reality.

As months passed, Clara expanded Sophie's abilities. She added new workflows for rental inquiries, mortgage consultations, document reminders, and property updates. She connected Sophie to her marketing system so every high-quality caller automatically received a follow-up message. She trained Sophie on complex scenarios that used to overwhelm human assistants. The agent adapted, improved, and learned faster than any employee Clara had ever hired. Sophie had become the backbone of her business—loyal, tireless, accurate, and endlessly helpful.

One evening, as Clara locked up her office, she glanced at her phone. Sophie had just answered a call from a first-time homebuyer. Clara listened to the recorded interaction later. Sophie's tone was warm. Her questions were thoughtful. Her guidance was clear. She didn't rush. She didn't hesitate. She didn't stumble. She simply delivered perfect service, exactly as Clara had designed her to do. In that moment, Clara understood the true power of voice AI: it wasn't about replacing people—it was about finally giving small business owners the support they deserved. Sophie wasn't just a tool. She was the assistant who never slept, never complained, and never failed.

And she had changed everything.

Chapter 2

Designing Natural Voice Conversations

Designing a great voice AI agent begins with understanding how people naturally speak. Unlike typed conversations, voice interactions rely heavily on flow, timing, tone, and clarity. When a caller says something, they expect the agent to respond immediately and naturally, without long pauses or robotic delays. The goal is to create a conversation that feels intuitive. To accomplish this, you must design your prompts and responses to mimic the patterns of human conversation. Good voice design avoids complexity, reduces friction, and guides callers smoothly through each step of the interaction. Before you ever drag a block inside Voiceflow or choose a voice inside ElevenLabs, you need to map out how a real human would talk, respond, and guide the user. This chapter teaches you exactly how to construct those conversations so your AI agent feels effortless and human-like.

The first rule of voice design is simplicity. Humans speak in short, clear bursts—not long, overly detailed paragraphs. A good AI voice agent uses concise prompts, friendly phrases, and guided questions. For example, instead of saying, “In order to better facilitate this process, could you provide me with the complete details of your inquiry today?” the agent should simply say, “How can I help you today?” Simplicity builds trust. It also helps callers feel comfortable speaking freely rather than feeling interrogated by a machine. When prompts are too long, callers interrupt or get confused. When prompts are too vague, callers are unsure what to say. The ideal conversation flow sits squarely in the middle: short, clear, warm, and direct.

Another key concept in voice design is *turn-taking*. Humans naturally alternate turns when speaking. When one person talks, the other listens. If the AI agent cuts the caller off or responds too quickly, the conversation feels unnatural. If it waits too long, the caller thinks something is broken. Voiceflow allows you to fine-tune this timing. You can add small pauses to make the agent sound thoughtful. You can adjust the pacing of the script so the AI sounds patient rather than rushed. You can structure questions so the caller never feels overwhelmed or confused. Good turn-taking is one of the most important elements in making your AI feel alive rather than mechanical.

One of the most overlooked aspects of voice AI design is expectation-setting. When a real human receptionist answers the phone, they often explain what they will do next. Voice agents need to do the same. If your agent is about to check the calendar, it should say, “Let me check that for you.” If it is about to gather information, it might say, “I’ll ask you a few quick questions." If it needs a moment to process something, it can say, "One second while I look that up." These micro-phrases eliminate confusion and help callers understand what is happening behind the scenes. Without them, callers may interrupt, repeat themselves, or assume the agent is malfunctioning. Clear expectations build comfort and confidence.

Designing believable voice AI also requires strong handling of errors and misunderstandings. Human callers don't always answer questions clearly. They may speak too fast, give incomplete information, or mention multiple ideas at once. In these moments, your agent must remain calm, polite, and in control. Instead of repeating a question verbatim, it should rephrase slightly or offer guidance. Instead of immediately escalating to a human, it should attempt gentle clarification. Voiceflow allows you to design fallback prompts and error handlers that guide callers back on track. These moments of confusion are where great voice agents truly stand out, because a smooth recovery feels incredibly human.

Finally, great voice design incorporates *personality*. This is not the same as adding jokes or unnecessary flair. Personality is about consistency in tone and attitude. Is your agent warm and friendly? Professional and direct? Calm and reassuring? Energetic and enthusiastic? You must decide on a single personality and apply it across every phrase it speaks. ElevenLabs enables you to choose or create a voice that matches your desired personality. Voiceflow enables you to embed tone and emotional direction in your scripts. When voice, tone, and phrasing all align, the result is an agent that feels intentional and trustworthy. Consistent personality transforms your voice agent from a tool into a meaningful part of your business identity.

By mastering natural conversation design, you give your AI agent the ability to not only speak—but to *connect*. And this connection is what leads callers to trust, follow instructions, complete tasks, and walk away satisfied. As you continue through this book, every design decision will build on these foundations: simplicity, clarity, natural pacing, expectation-setting, error handling, and consistent personality. Together, these elements create voice experiences that feel less like technology and more like a genuine human interaction. Once you understand how these pieces fit together, building powerful voice AI agents becomes not just possible—but truly exciting.

"The Voice That Knew Exactly What to Say"

Elias owned a busy dental clinic in a growing neighborhood. His biggest challenge wasn't attracting new patients—it was managing the constant stream of appointments, cancellations, questions, and last-minute emergencies. His receptionist, Ana, was excellent, but she was overwhelmed. Patients called at all hours, many leaving frustrated voicemails when the office was closed. Elias hated the idea of patients feeling ignored, but he couldn't justify hiring a second full-time employee. One night, after yet another stressful week, he decided to test something he had heard about but never considered seriously—voice AI.

He installed Voiceflow, connected it to a temporary phone line, and created a basic flow. The first version of his AI receptionist, whom he named "Mila," was functional but stiff. She answered calls promptly but sounded like a monotone robot reading from a script. Elias almost gave up, but something told him to keep going. He dug deeper into tutorials, experimented with conversational flows, adjusted the timing, simplified questions, and changed her ElevenLabs voice to something warm and soothing. Slowly, the transformation began. Mila started to sound less like a machine and more like someone who genuinely cared about helping.

When Mila finally went live, she greeted callers with a friendly, "Hi, this is Mila with GreenLeaf Dental. How can I help you today?" Her tone was warm, confident, and composed. She asked clear questions, such as, "What day works best for your appointment?" and "Would you prefer mornings or afternoons?" She guided callers step by step, pausing naturally when they spoke and responding with surprising fluidity. Patients who spoke quickly, nervously, or emotionally were handled with gentle reassurance. After a full day of calls, Elias listened to the audio logs with astonishment. Mila handled scheduling better than any assistant he had ever hired.

The real breakthrough came one afternoon when a patient named Mrs. Gomez called in tears because her son had chipped a tooth at school. Her voice trembled as she explained what happened. Mila responded with calm confidence, saying, "I'm here to help. I'll get you the next available emergency appointment. One moment while I check the schedule." Her tone slowed down, providing comfort without sounding artificial. When Mrs. Gomez gave details chaotically, Mila gently clarified them. When she paused, overwhelmed, Mila guided her forward. By the time the appointment was booked, Mrs. Gomez thanked Mila repeatedly—believing she had spoken to a real, compassionate assistant.

Elias watched this interaction with disbelief. How could a system made of code and prompts understand emotion so well? How could a voice generated by AI respond with such empathy? The truth, he realized, was that natural conversation design wasn't about pretending to be human—it was about being helpful. By crafting prompts with intention, aligning tone with purpose, and designing for clarity, he had created an agent capable of meeting people where they were emotionally, not just informationally.

The days that followed confirmed this transformation. Patients commented on how polite "the new receptionist" was. They loved that she never rushed them. They loved that she repeated details gently when needed. They loved that she always knew exactly what to say. Some even brought boxes of chocolates to the office for Mila—completely unaware she wasn't real. Elias shared these stories with his staff, who laughed and shook their heads, amazed.

By the end of the month, something unexpected happened: the office felt calmer. Patients were happier. Ana, the human receptionist, felt supported rather than overwhelmed. Elias had built an assistant who never grew tired, never became impatient, and never lost her composure. And all of it was possible because he had learned how to design conversations that felt natural, comforting, and genuinely helpful.

Mila wasn't just answering phones. She was building trust—one beautifully crafted conversation at a time.

Chapter 3

Choosing the Right Voice Personality

Every great voice AI agent begins with a clearly defined personality. This personality shapes how callers feel, how they respond, and how deeply they trust the agent. Choosing a voice personality is more than selecting a tone or style—it is about intentionally crafting the emotional experience your callers will have. Human assistants are judged by the warmth of their greetings, the clarity of their explanations, and the confidence in their tone. Your voice AI agent must reflect these same qualities, but in a consistent and predictable way across every interaction. A strong voice personality anchors the agent's behavior, wording, rhythm, energy, and overall presence, making every conversation feel deliberate rather than mechanical. This chapter will help you choose and design that personality with precision.

The first step in building a voice personality is identifying the purpose of the agent. A voice agent meant for customer support should sound calm, empathetic, and patient. A sales agent may benefit from sounding upbeat, friendly, and confident. A medical assistant should sound reassuring, professional, and steady. A real estate agent may take on a warm and conversational tone to make clients feel welcome. The personality must match the job. When callers interact with your agent, the tone should immediately communicate competence and emotional alignment. If the personality conflicts with the task—for example, a cheerful tone in a financial emergency hotline—the agent will feel unnatural and may even cause trust issues.

Once the purpose is established, the next step is choosing the tone characteristics: warmth, speed, energy, confidence, and friendliness. Warmth makes callers feel safe. Speed determines pacing—slower tones are ideal for complex or emotional conversations, while faster tones work well for logistics and scheduling. Energy determines how lively or subdued the agent feels. Confidence is essential in scenarios where the caller depends on the agent for guidance. Friendliness makes the experience feel approachable. These dimensions allow you to shape the emotional texture of every interaction. When combined thoughtfully, they give your AI voice a clear identity that callers recognize instantly.

After defining tone, you must consider linguistic style. This includes the type of phrasing your agent uses. Does it speak in short, simple sentences or more structured formal language? Does it offer reassurances like "I can help with that" or keep communication strictly informational? Does it use contractions like "I'll" and "let's" to feel conversational, or does it remain precise and exact? Small differences in language create big differences in how people perceive the agent. A conversational agent feels friendly. A formal agent feels authoritative. A directive agent feels efficient. No style is right or wrong—the key is choosing one and using it consistently. Consistency creates the illusion of personality.

The next step is selecting the voice itself, and modern tools like ElevenLabs make this incredibly flexible. You can choose from pre-built voices or create fully custom ones. You can adjust vocal clarity, age, accent, and emotional tone. You can even clone your own voice if you want your business to have a personal touch. When selecting a voice, focus on matching it to your personality guidelines. A friendly, warm personality needs a smooth, approachable voice. A high-authority personality may require a deeper, more stable tone. A fast-paced logistics assistant might benefit from a brighter, more energetic voice. The voice is not chosen for beauty—it is chosen for purpose.

Finally, you must ensure that the personality is implemented consistently throughout the entire conversation flow. This includes the introduction, questions, confirmations, clarifications, fallback prompts, and closing statements. If the agent is calm and patient in one moment but abrupt in another, the illusion breaks. Your scripts must reflect the personality at every turn. Phrases like “No problem, let me check that for you," "I'm here to help," or "Take your time" all help maintain tone. Meanwhile, avoiding extremes—like overly enthusiastic or overly formal lines—keeps the personality grounded. The more consistent the voice personality is, the more natural the agent feels.

By choosing the right voice personality, you give your AI agent a soul—something callers can emotionally connect to. The personality becomes a familiar presence, one that callers learn to trust. And as your business grows, your voice agent becomes part of your brand identity: recognizable, reliable, and memorable. A well-crafted personality is not just a design choice—it is a competitive advantage.

"The Voice Customers Fell in Love With"

When Maya opened her wellness clinic, she wanted every client who walked through the door to feel calm, welcomed, and understood. But she struggled with the same problem that plagues many small businesses: phones ringing constantly, callers asking anxious questions, and new clients needing guidance at all hours. She dreamed of a receptionist who embodied the clinic's peaceful atmosphere, someone with a soothing voice who could comfort nervous callers before they ever stepped foot inside. But hiring someone with that perfect presence was expensive—and often impossible. She needed something better. Something she could shape completely to match her brand.

That's when she discovered voice AI. Maya was skeptical at first. She didn't want a robotic voice representing her clinic. She wanted warmth, patience, and emotional intelligence. But as she explored ElevenLabs' voice library, she heard something that made her stop scrolling—a gentle, calming female voice with soft edges and perfect pacing. The moment she heard it, she felt something click. "This is her," Maya whispered. "This is the voice my clinic has been missing." She named the agent "Liora," meaning "light," because the voice sounded like a warm sunrise.

Maya spent days crafting the personality behind the voice. She wanted Liora to sound compassionate, supportive, and grounded. Every phrase was rewritten to reflect kindness. Instead of saying, "Please provide your appointment date," Liora said, "Whenever you're ready, could you tell me what day works best for you?" Instead of, "Invalid response," she said, "No worries, let's try that again." Maya gave Liora the exact emotional energy she wished she had time to give every caller herself. She created scripts that felt reassuring, added pauses that made Liora sound thoughtful, and avoided any language that felt rushed or demanding. The first time Liora answered a real call, Maya listened closely. A new client named Daniella called, speaking in a shaky voice because she was nervous about her upcoming treatment. Liora responded with a warm, steady tone, immediately shifting the emotional atmosphere. "You're in good hands," she said gently. "Let's help you get everything set up." As Daniella answered questions, her voice softened. By the end of the call, she thanked Liora as though she had spoken to a caring human. Maya could hardly believe what she was hearing. She felt tears forming—not because the system worked, but because it gave her clients the comfort she always wanted to provide.

As weeks went by, the reaction became almost predictable. Clients began complimenting "the receptionist with the beautiful voice." Some said they looked forward to calling. Others said Liora helped them feel calm during stressful moments. One client, dealing with chronic anxiety, told Maya that hearing Liora's voice helped them feel grounded. "Whoever she is," they said, "she's incredible." Maya smiled but didn't correct them. Liora wasn't just a tool anymore—she was part of the heart of the clinic.

As demand grew, Liora handled scheduling, follow-ups, FAQ calls, and appointment reminders. She never forgot details. She never rushed anyone. She never judged. Her tone remained consistent, day after day, conversation after conversation. Maya watched her business transform. No more overwhelmed staff. No more missed calls. No more anxious clients feeling alone. Liora had become the emotional anchor of the clinic. And every time Maya listened to the call recordings, she felt grateful for the moment she chose the right voice—the moment she realized that personality isn't optional. It's the soul of the experience.

Liora didn't just represent the wellness clinic. She embodied it. Through her voice, clients felt peace, comfort, and safety—exactly what Maya had always dreamed of offering.

Chapter 4

Mapping the Conversation Flow in Voiceflow

Once you've chosen your agent's personality, the next step is turning that personality into a structured, intelligent conversation flow. Voiceflow is the ideal tool for this because it allows you to design interactions visually. Instead of writing code, you create a roadmap of how each conversation should unfold. Mapping the flow gives your voice agent clarity, consistency, and direction. Without a clearly planned flow, even the best-sounding voice will get confused, stuck, or repetitive. This chapter will guide you through designing professional-grade conversation maps that handle real callers and real business scenarios smoothly from start to finish.

The foundation of a strong conversation flow begins with the *entry point.* This is your agent's first impression. It includes the greeting, any brand-specific introduction, and the opening question that captures the caller's intent. A great entry point immediately sets the tone, establishes trust, and clarifies the purpose of the call. Voiceflow makes this easy by allowing you to create a "Start" block and connect it to a "Speak" block where your agent introduces itself. The opening question should be short, welcoming, and direct. Something as simple as "How can I help you today?" can open a clean path for any type of conversation.

After capturing the caller's intent, you must design *intent branches.* In Voiceflow, this is where your agent recognizes different categories of questions or actions. For example, if your agent handles appointments, FAQs, new inquiries, or emergencies, each category becomes its own branch. This method ensures your agent never feels lost. Voiceflow's intent blocks allow you to list expected phrases—like "I want to book an appointment" or "I have a question"—and route callers to the correct part of the flow. Properly defining intents is one of the most important parts of building a voice agent that feels intelligent rather than mechanical.

Once intents are mapped, you move to *dialogue sequences.* These are the step-by-step conversations inside each branch. For appointments, this may include choosing a date, confirming a time, and collecting necessary details. For support calls, this may include identifying the issue, providing instructions, and determining whether escalation is needed. A strong dialogue sequence prevents confusion by controlling the flow of questions and responses. Each step should end with a clear question that guides the caller naturally to the next step. Voiceflow's visual interface allows you to create these sequences by chaining together speak blocks, capture blocks, logic blocks, and integrations.

Another essential part of mapping your conversation is handling *fallbacks and misunderstandings*. Even the best-designed flows will encounter situations where callers say things the agent doesn't expect. This is why your map must include alternate paths: clarifying questions, gentle corrections, and graceful backup options. Voiceflow's "No Match" and "No Input" blocks help you redirect the caller smoothly without breaking the experience. These safety nets prevent the agent from sounding confused or repeating itself. They ensure your agent remains composed and helpful, regardless of how unpredictable the caller may be.

Next, you should integrate *actions and automations*. This is where your agent becomes truly useful. Voiceflow allows you to connect external tools directly into your map. You can integrate Google Sheets, CRMs, calendars, email platforms, Make.com workflows, and more. Each integration becomes a new branch in the flow. For example, once a caller chooses a date, the agent can automatically check the calendar. Once they provide details, the agent can store them in a CRM. These automations turn your voice agent into a worker that actually does something—not just talks. Mapping these integrations clearly helps prevent errors and guarantees smooth operation. Lastly, you must design a strong *closing flow*. This is the final impression your agent leaves. A professional closing includes confirming tasks, thanking the caller, and providing reassurance or next steps. Something simple like "I've scheduled your appointment. You'll receive a confirmation shortly. Thank you for calling—have a wonderful day" makes the agent feel polished and complete. Voiceflow allows you to create consistent closings across all branches. When a conversation ends with clarity and warmth, callers walk away satisfied and confident in your business.

Mapping a conversation flow in Voiceflow is like directing a play: every line, every movement, every transition must be intentional. When done correctly, the result is a voice agent that feels natural, capable, and reliable—an assistant callers feel comfortable trusting. With this framework, the next chapters will teach you how to add depth, intelligence, creativity, and automation to the flows you design.

"The Blueprint That Changed Everything"

Jordan owned a growing auto repair shop, but the rapid growth created chaos. Calls constantly flooded the office—customers needing quotes, asking about repairs, scheduling appointments, and panicking about noises coming from their cars. His receptionist tried her best, but she was overwhelmed. Customers were frustrated. Jordan was frustrated. Then one day, after a friend mentioned AI voice agents, he discovered Voiceflow. He didn't know it yet, but this discovery would change how his entire business operated.

He signed up and stared at the blank canvas on his screen. It felt intimidating at first. He wasn't a programmer. He didn't understand technical diagrams. But as he dragged his first "Speak" block onto the canvas, everything started making sense. Voiceflow didn't require code—it required logic. It required understanding how people talked to his business. Jordan suddenly realized he wasn't building software. He was designing conversations he had experienced thousands of times over the years. And nobody understood those conversations better than he did.

He began by mapping out the greeting: warm, friendly, and confident, just like he wanted every customer interaction to feel. Then he created the first branching paths. One branch for quotes. One for scheduling. One for checking repair status. One for emergency calls. As he dragged the pathways onto the canvas, it felt like he was finally organizing the chaos that had overwhelmed him for so long. For the first time, he could see how every customer conversation fit together like puzzle pieces.

Jordan added questions that felt natural. "Can you tell me the make and model of your car?" "When would you like to come in?" "Is the issue happening constantly or only sometimes?" He added logic conditions so the AI could ask deeper questions when needed. He added fallbacks for unclear answers. He built paths that guided frantic callers with calm, step-by-step instructions. As the map grew more detailed, he felt a strange sense of relief. It was as if he was finally building the perfect version of a receptionist—one who never forgot details, never got overwhelmed, and always knew what to say.

But the true breakthrough came when Jordan connected his flows to real actions. Using integrations, he made the agent check available repair bays. He connected it to his scheduling system so it could book appointments instantly. He linked it to a Google Sheet that stored customer information. Now the agent wasn't just answering questions—it was doing work. Actual work. Work that used to consume hours of Jordan's day. Forty phone calls that once felt like a nightmare now became smooth, predictable workflows.

The day he turned the agent on, Jordan sat back and listened. A customer called, panicked because her car wouldn't start. The agent greeted her gently, asked the right questions, and offered the earliest available time. When she accepted, the appointment was automatically added to the calendar. She thanked the agent, completely unaware she hadn't spoken to a human. Jordan stared at the call log in disbelief. It worked. It really worked. Over the next week, the transformation became undeniable. His receptionist no longer looked exhausted. Customers stopped complaining about being put on hold. Appointments doubled because the AI handled them instantly. Jordan finally had time to focus on expanding the business instead of constantly fighting fires. He realized that mapping the conversation in Voiceflow hadn't just built a voice agent. It had built structure. Stability. Freedom.

One night, as he reviewed the latest call recordings, Jordan smiled. He could hear the results of his work—clarity, order, and confidence in every conversation. For the first time, his business wasn't reacting to chaos. It was running with precision. And it all started with the blueprint he created in Voiceflow.

Chapter 5

Integrating ElevenLabs for Natural, Human-Like Voice Output

To bring your voice agent to life, you must give it a voice that feels natural, trustworthy, and emotionally aligned with your brand. ElevenLabs is the leading tool for generating ultra-realistic AI voices, and integrating it with your Voiceflow agent dramatically elevates the entire experience. A strong script and well-designed conversation flow are essential, but without the right voice, the agent will still feel artificial. ElevenLabs solves this by producing voices with human-like tone, pitch, warmth, pacing, emotion, and nuance. In this chapter, you will learn how to select, refine, test, and integrate ElevenLabs voices into your no-code phone agent so every interaction feels like it's coming from a real professional assistant.

The first step is choosing the right voice model. ElevenLabs offers a library of diverse voices across genders, ages, accents, and emotional ranges. You can preview each one, listen for tone and clarity, and pick the voice that best reflects your agent's personality. For example, a finance agent may require a confident, steady voice. A wellness assistant might benefit from a soft, calming voice. A sales agent may need an energetic, upbeat tone. The selection process should be intentional, guided by the brand identity and the emotional impact you want callers to feel. Once you choose a base voice, ElevenLabs allows custom configuration of stability, clarity, and similarity, giving you precise control over how expressive the voice should sound.

Next, you must focus on consistency. ElevenLabs gives you the power to standardize your agent's voice across all responses, meaning every phrase the AI speaks will follow the same vocal profile. This ensures that callers experience a unified personality throughout their conversation. Consistency builds trust because the voice never fluctuates, never loses tone, and never introduces emotional unpredictability. If your agent helps with sensitive topics like billing, medical support, or legal tasks, a calm and consistent voice is especially important. Even for simple tasks like scheduling or answering FAQs, consistency creates a polished, professional experience callers immediately recognize and appreciate.

Once the voice is chosen, the next step is testing. Before integrating the voice with Voiceflow, you should generate sample lines from your script to hear how they sound. ElevenLabs allows you to input text and preview the audio instantly. This is where you refine pacing, emotional tone, and phrasing. Sometimes a line looks great on paper but feels awkward when spoken aloud. Testing helps you identify opportunities to simplify, clarify, or adjust your script for optimal vocal delivery. It also helps you hear whether your chosen personality truly comes through in the voice. If not, you can adjust the stability settings or try a different voice altogether.

When you are ready to integrate the voice into Voiceflow, ElevenLabs provides an API endpoint that you can connect directly using the "HTTP Request" block. This allows Voiceflow to send text to ElevenLabs and receive audio output dynamically. You can configure the request to include your chosen voice model, stability settings, and API key. Voiceflow will then use the audio returned by ElevenLabs in real time during the phone conversation. This integration creates fluid, responsive voice interactions that feel natural to callers. Once the connection is set, every Speak block in your flow can route through ElevenLabs, ensuring every phrase your agent speaks arrives in the exact tone and style you designed.

Finally, you should optimize your scripts specifically for spoken audio. Written text does not always translate well into spoken dialogue. ElevenLabs voices sound best when the text is conversational, concise, and structured with natural pauses. Add commas where pauses should occur. Avoid overly long sentences that can overwhelm callers. Use contractions to make speech sound less formal. Substitute complicated vocabulary for simpler words when possible. The goal is to craft dialogue that feels effortless to listen to. When your script and voice are perfectly aligned, the agent comes alive in a way that surprises callers—it feels warm, intelligent, and genuinely human.

Integrating ElevenLabs into your workflow transforms your voice agent from a functional tool into a polished professional presence. With the right voice, the right pacing, and the right emotional resonance, your agent becomes a true representative of your brand—someone callers feel comfortable talking to and trusting. Voice AI is powerful, but voice AI with ElevenLabs is unforgettable.

"The Voice That Won Every Caller's Trust"

Julia ran a small tax preparation service that became overwhelmed every year during the busy season. Her clients were stressed, anxious, and often scared about deadlines or mistakes. Many called with shaky voices, worried about audits or confused about paperwork. Julia wanted someone who could answer calls warmly, reassure clients, and gather details patiently. But she couldn't afford another full-time employee, and temporary workers felt rushed or detached. When she heard about voice AI, she was intrigued—but she knew one thing for certain: if the voice didn't sound truly human, it would only make her clients more nervous.

She signed up for ElevenLabs and began exploring the voice options. Some voices sounded too robotic. Others felt too cheerful. But then she heard one particular voice—a gentle, thoughtful female tone with soft edges and perfect pacing. Something about it made her smile. It reminded her of her grandmother, who used to soothe her during difficult times. In that moment, Julia knew she had found the right voice. She named the AI "Elena," imagining her as a calm, steady presence who could help clients breathe easier during stressful tax situations.

Julia spent hours crafting Elena's dialogue and testing how it sounded through ElevenLabs. She typed lines like "I'm here to help you sort this out" and "Let's take this step by step," and each time she listened, she felt warmth spread through her chest. Elena sounded real—not overly emotional, not artificial, but genuinely comforting. When she adjusted the stability setting slightly higher, Elena's tone became even more steady, perfect for anxious callers. Julia recorded sample calls and played them for her husband, who asked, surprised, "Who did you hire?" She laughed. "No one. That's our new voice AI."

When Elena finally went live, Julia held her breath. The first call came from a man named Thomas, whose tone carried frustration and fear. His tax documents were overdue, and he didn't know what to do. Elena answered with calm precision: "Hi, this is Elena. I'm here to help you. Tell me what you're dealing with, and we'll figure it out together." Thomas exhaled loudly—Julia could hear the relief in his voice. He explained his situation in a rush, but Elena responded without a hint of panic. She collected details gently, repeated key information clearly, and reassured him after each step. By the end of the call, Thomas sounded lighter. "Thank you," he said softly. "I really needed that."

Word spread quickly. Clients called the office praising this "amazing new assistant." Some asked if Elena could help them specifically because they liked her voice. Others said she made tax season feel less overwhelming. One elderly client, who usually avoided phone calls, said Elena made her feel safe enough to explain everything without embarrassment. Julia realized something profound: this wasn't just a voice. This was emotional support. Trust. Stability. Something her business had been missing for years.

As the season continued, Elena handled hundreds of calls flawlessly. She never sounded tired. Never impatient. Never irritated. Even during the busiest weeks, the office felt peaceful—a drastic change from past years. Julia watched call logs fill with smooth, successful interactions and felt gratitude every time she listened to recordings of Elena's gentle, steady tone guiding clients through complicated issues.

One evening, long after closing time, Julia sat alone in the office and replayed a recording of Elena helping a panicked college student file taxes for the first time. Elena's voice was calming and encouraging: "You're doing great. I'll guide you through the rest." It struck Julia that this was the voice she had always wished she could give every client—the voice of reassurance she didn't always have time to offer herself.

Elena didn't just make the business more efficient. She made it more human. And thanks to ElevenLabs, Julia had built a voice her clients trusted completely.

Chapter 6

Connecting Your Voice Agent to a Phone System Using Twilio or Aircall

Once your voice agent has a personality, a mapped conversation flow, and a realistic ElevenLabs voice, the next step is giving it the ability to handle real phone calls. This is where Twilio and Aircall come in. These platforms provide the telephony infrastructure that allows your AI agent to receive calls, make calls, route calls, and engage with callers exactly the way a human receptionist would. Without a phone integration, your agent is only a simulation. With the right setup, it becomes a fully automated call-handling system that can operate twenty-four hours a day. This chapter walks you through connecting your Voiceflow agent to Twilio or Aircall so you can transform your AI assistant into a real, functional phone agent.

The first step is choosing your platform. Twilio is ideal for builders who want flexibility, customization, and global coverage. It offers programmable voice capabilities, phone numbers in dozens of countries, call forwarding, caller ID configuration, and automated workflows. Aircall is best for businesses that want a polished, ready-to-use phone system with advanced call center features, team routing, voicemail boxes, analytics, and CRM integrations. Both platforms work seamlessly with Voiceflow, but your choice should reflect your goals. If you want granular control, Twilio is the way to go. If you want ease and speed, Aircall is perfect.

After selecting your platform, you need to secure a phone number. In Twilio, you can purchase a number directly inside the dashboard by searching for local, toll-free, or international options. Once purchased, you can configure the number to use a webhook—the URL where Twilio will send incoming calls. Voiceflow generates this webhook once you publish your agent. In Aircall, the process is even easier; you select a number from their library and connect it to a flow using their visual routing interface. Either way, your AI agent will soon have its own dedicated phone number, ready to answer calls from real people.

Next, you must connect the incoming call to Voiceflow. In Twilio, this is done through TwiML, a markup language that tells Twilio what to do with a call. You simply instruct Twilio to forward audio to your Voiceflow webhook. Voiceflow receives the audio, processes it through speech-to-text, responds via ElevenLabs-generated speech, and sends the audio back to Twilio to play for the caller. In Aircall, you route the call to a Voiceflow integration by selecting your agent as the call destination. The process is designed to be beginner-friendly, allowing you to focus on the agent's behavior rather than the technical backend.

Once the connection is active, it's time to test your agent in the real world. Place a call from your phone and listen to the greeting. Does the voice play at the right speed? Is there any delay? Do the responses sound clear? Does the agent correctly capture information when you speak naturally rather than with scripted phrases? Testing real calls is essential because phone audio is compressed differently than web-based playback. If the audio levels are off, you may need to adjust your ElevenLabs settings or your Voiceflow audio configuration. This stage is all about fine-tuning the natural feel of your phone agent.

As you finalize the system, you can begin adding advanced call-handling logic. Twilio allows you to forward calls to humans when needed, route calls based on time of day, block spam, record calls, or even send SMS messages during conversations. Aircall allows for team routing, call tagging, analytics, voicemail transcriptions, and CRM synchronization. These features let you build a call-handling system far more powerful and consistent than any traditional receptionist desk. And because everything is automated, the agent can handle unlimited calls at once—something even the best human teams can't do.

Connecting your agent to a phone system completes the transformation from concept to reality. Once Twilio or Aircall is integrated, your voice AI agent becomes a living part of your business—one that never sleeps, never misses a call, and never fails to deliver consistent service. With this step, you have moved from building a prototype to deploying a full operational solution. The next chapters will teach you how to enhance this system even further, turning your voice agent into one of the most powerful assets your business has ever seen.

"The First Call That Changed the Entire Business"

For months, Marco had been building his AI voice agent late at night after running his busy landscaping company all day. His phone rang constantly—customers asking for quotes, changing appointments, requesting emergency visits, or simply needing reassurance. His small team couldn't keep up. Calls were missed. Opportunities slipped away. Frustration grew. Marco needed help, but hiring another receptionist felt impossible. When he discovered voice AI, he found hope. But it wasn't until he connected his agent to a real phone number that everything changed.

He decided to use Twilio because he wanted complete control. He bought a number—305-555-0198—and configured it to point to his Voiceflow webhook. His heart raced as he saved the settings. The AI wasn't just a project anymore. It was about to pick up real calls. He stared at the screen for a moment, then reached for his cell phone. With a deep breath, he dialed the number and waited. A moment later, he heard the voice he had crafted so carefully: warm, confident, and unmistakably human.

"Hi, this is Luna with GreenVine Landscaping. How can I help you today?" Marco froze. Hearing the words through an actual telephone line sent chills through him. This was real. Luna wasn't a project; she was the new voice of his business. He tested her responses, speaking casually, even mumbling. She captured every detail. She asked follow-up questions exactly as he had designed. She scheduled a pretend appointment and sent a confirmation message through an automated workflow. Marco couldn't believe it. He had just created an employee who worked instantly, flawlessly, and without ever asking for a break.

The real test came two days later, when a storm hit the city and dozens of customers needed emergency cleanup. Calls poured in. Normally, this kind of day would overwhelm the entire company. But this time, things were different. Luna answered every call with the same calm professionalism. She filtered callers based on urgency, collected photos through a link she texted them, checked crew availability through a Google Sheet integration, and scheduled emergency visits instantly. She didn't panic when multiple calls came at once. She didn't put anyone on hold. She didn't miss a single customer. Marco and his team finished their work, drenched from the rain but amazed at the efficiency. The next day, he checked the call logs. Luna had handled sixty-three calls in a single afternoon. Sixty-three. And every one of them led to clear, organized appointments, detailed notes, and zero confusion. Marco sat at his desk staring at the numbers. Luna had done the impossible. She had done the work of five people without breaking a sweat. His business had survived the storm—not because he was lucky, but because he had built something powerful.

Over the next weeks, customers began praising "the new receptionist" who always sounded so kind and never rushed anyone. One client said, "She must be the most patient person in the world." Marco smiled and said nothing. People were building relationships with Luna without realizing she wasn't human. She had become the voice they trusted, the calm presence that reassured them their property was in good hands.

Late one night, Marco replayed the first official call Luna ever took. He sat in the quiet office, listening to her gentle greeting echo through the speakers. He remembered the nerves, the doubt, the hours spent learning Twilio and Voiceflow. Now, everything had paid off. That first call had changed the trajectory of his entire business. Luna wasn't just an AI agent—she was the reason his company finally operated with ease instead of chaos.

And she had answered that very first call like she had been doing it her entire life.

Chapter 7

Training Your Agent to Understand Caller Intent Accurately

Even the most beautifully designed voice agent will fail if it cannot correctly understand what callers mean. Caller intent is the core of every conversation. It determines how your agent interprets questions, responds appropriately, and moves callers through the right flow. Because callers speak freely—using different vocabulary, emotions, pacing, or accents—your AI agent must be trained to recognize patterns, interpret meaning, and react correctly regardless of how the caller phrases their request. This chapter will show you how to train your voice agent to detect intent with precision, ensuring that every caller ends up exactly where they need to be.

The first step in training intent recognition is identifying the main categories of requests your callers make. These are your intent buckets. For example, a medical office may have intents like "Book appointment," "Cancel appointment," "Ask about billing," or "Medication question." A law firm might have intents like "Schedule consultation," "Case update," or "Urgent callback." Your job is to map these categories based on real business needs. Once you establish your intent buckets, your agent has a framework for understanding conversation direction. Without these categories, your agent would treat every input the same way, leading to confusion and misrouting.

Once categories are defined, you must provide example utterances for each intent. These are samples of what a caller might say. For example, the intent "Book appointment" might include utterances like "I need to schedule something," "I want to come in," "I need an appointment," "When is the next available time?" or "Can I book a visit?" Voiceflow uses these sample utterances to teach the AI how this intent sounds across different phrasing styles. The more variations you include, the smarter your agent becomes. You should gather real examples from your business—emails, voicemails, or live conversations—to capture authentic language patterns. This ensures your agent recognizes real-world phrasing, not just textbook versions.

Next, you must design fallback detection—the plan for when the agent isn't completely sure what the caller wants. Even with perfect training, callers will sometimes speak unclearly or introduce topics the agent isn't prepared for. This is where your fallback prompts come into play. A good fallback prompt is gentle and clarifying, such as "I want to help you with that. Can you tell me briefly what you're calling about?" This gives the caller another chance to provide clarity without feeling judged or dismissed. The fallback system should not feel robotic or repetitive. Instead, it should feel like a naturally patient assistant seeking understanding.

Another critical component is using contextual awareness. Voiceflow allows your agent to remember parts of the conversation and use that information to interpret new messages. If a caller previously mentioned an appointment, the agent can infer that later questions are likely related. If a caller mentioned "billing," follow-up questions are likely financial. This contextual memory gives your agent a more human-like understanding of continuity. Human assistants rely on context every day—your AI agent should too. When context is applied correctly, callers feel like the agent is truly listening rather than restarting the conversation repeatedly.

Once your intent system is in place, test it aggressively. Speak naturally, fast, slow, emotionally, or with background noise. Try accents. Try slang. Try fragmented phrases. Your agent must be tested under real conditions—not just perfect ones. Each failed recognition becomes data to improve your intents. Add new utterances, refine phrasing, and adjust categories as needed. Every test sharpens the system. After enough refinement, your AI agent will understand intent as well as a trained receptionist, and in many cases better—because it doesn't get confused, tired, or distracted. When your agent fully understands caller intent, it transforms from a scripted tool into a dynamic, intelligent assistant. Intent recognition allows the agent to route callers instantly, reduce misunderstandings, elevate user satisfaction, and maintain natural conversational flow. It also allows your entire automation system to work with precision, because correct routing is the foundation of accurate workflow execution. By mastering intent training, you unlock the full power of your voice AI agent.

"The Agent Who Always Understood"

Amina ran a small law office specializing in immigration cases, and almost every caller who reached out to her was stressed, confused, or navigating complex personal situations. Each phone conversation carried emotion—hope, fear, urgency, frustration, or uncertainty. When Amina decided to build a voice AI agent to help manage calls, she knew the agent had to do more than speak nicely. It had to understand what callers meant even when they didn't express it clearly. Missing intent wasn't an option. A confused agent could make a stressful situation worse. So Amina committed to training her AI meticulously, determined to create an assistant that truly understood her clients.

She started by listening to weeks' worth of past voicemails—dozens of callers each speaking differently. One person said, "I need help with my case." Another said, "I want to check on my paperwork." Another whispered, "Is my appointment still happening?" Someone else simply said, "I need to talk to someone." Each message taught her something important: people rarely say exactly what they mean. Their emotions shape their words. Their backgrounds shape their phrasing. Their urgency shapes their tone. Amina saw patterns emerging, and slowly she formed intent categories—case updates, new consultations, document issues, court date questions, and emergencies.

She added dozens of utterances to each category, typing real phrases word for word. She didn't sanitize the language. She kept the pauses, the fragmented questions, the uncertainty. She taught her agent how people *actually* speak—not how textbooks say they speak. As the list grew, she felt a deeper connection to her clients. This wasn't just building an AI. It was building a digital ear that understood the lives of the people she served.

When she tested the agent for the first time, she pretended to be a nervous caller. "Uh... I need to ask about my... um... the thing I filed," she stammered. The agent responded calmly, "Are you asking for an update on your immigration documents?" Amina's eyes widened. It understood. She tried again, using a different tone, pretending to cry through the words. The agent understood again. It even adapted its tone gently, offering patient follow-up questions. It didn't need perfect grammar. It didn't require clarity. It recognized her meaning through fragments. The real test came when the first live caller reached the agent. A man called in a panic, speaking quickly in accented English. "My case—my deadline—I don't know what to do," he rushed out. The agent immediately identified his intent as "urgent case support" and responded, "I'm here to help. First, I'll collect a few details. Then I'll guide you." His pace slowed. His breathing steadied. The agent understood him instantly—even though no human receptionist could have deciphered his rushed expression that quickly.

Over the next month, Amina listened to call logs with awe. Her agent understood callers who rambled, callers who whispered, callers who didn't know the right words, callers who were embarrassed, callers who switched languages mid-sentence. The agent never judged, never rushed, and never misinterpreted their needs. Every recognition was precise. Every response was appropriate. It routed callers effortlessly, making each one feel heard.

One morning, an elderly woman called speaking softly, barely audible. "I... I think I... I need... someone... to help me..." she murmured. The agent responded gently, "Are you calling to schedule a consultation? I can help you with that." The woman gasped softly. "Yes... thank you... yes, that's what I need." Amina felt tears in her eyes. Her agent didn't just understand language—it understood people. From that moment forward, she realized she hadn't just built a tool. She had built a bridge—something that listened with clarity, responded with intelligence, and understood callers more accurately than any human assistant she had ever hired. Her agent didn't just recognize intent. It recognized emotion, context, and meaning.

It understood. And understanding made all the difference.

Chapter 8

Building Multi-Step Logic and Conditional Paths

Once your voice agent can understand intent, the next major upgrade is teaching it how to think through multi-step decisions. Multi-step logic is what allows your agent to handle complex tasks that require several layers of information, branching options, and conditional outcomes. For example, scheduling an appointment requires checking dates, confirming availability, gathering caller details, and validating time slots. Handling billing questions requires identifying the issue, checking account information, and routing properly. Without conditional logic and multi-step sequences, your agent would be limited to simple responses. With these capabilities, it becomes a powerful automated problem solver capable of handling the kind of tasks human assistants perform every day.

To build multi-step flows in Voiceflow, begin by breaking the task into clear stages. Each stage becomes a "block" in your design. For example, a three-step identity verification flow might involve confirming the user's name, checking their date of birth, then retrieving their file. A good designer identifies each discrete step and determines what success or failure looks like. This clarity helps the agent move logically from one part of the process to the next. Once the steps are mapped, you can begin adding conditions using Voiceflow's logic blocks. Conditions allow your agent to compare the caller's answer with required rules—such as verifying whether a date is available, determining whether a caller qualifies for a service, or choosing different responses based on what the caller says.

Next, consider all possible outcomes at each decision point. Multi-step flows often require branches: what happens if the day requested is unavailable? What happens if the caller doesn't provide enough information? What happens if a detail contradicts earlier answers? Conditional logic allows you to structure these decision points so your agent remains adaptable and accurate. Every branch should have a clear purpose. If a condition fails, the agent should never freeze or sound confused. Instead, it should naturally redirect, using smooth fallback language such as "Let's try a different option." Planning for alternative outcomes ensures seamless experiences even when callers go off course.

Another important part of multi-step logic is using variables. In Voiceflow, variables allow the agent to store information and reuse it later in the conversation. For example, your agent can capture the caller's name, preferred service, appointment date, or issue description and reuse those details in later steps.

This makes the interaction feel deeply personal and human. Using variables also enables more advanced conditional statements—such as checking if the appointment time is available or if the caller has given all necessary information. Variables are the memory system that transforms your agent from reactive to proactive.

Testing multi-step flows is essential. As the number of branches grows, so does the potential for small mistakes. You must run through every path, every branch, and every fallback option. Speak naturally, interrupt the agent, give partial answers, and make mistakes intentionally. The more chaotic your testing, the more resilient your agent becomes. Multi-step agents thrive when designed under real-world pressure, not perfect test conditions. When every branch works, every fallback triggers correctly, and every variable is stored accurately, the agent becomes a reliable partner capable of handling complexity.

Finally, remember that multi-step logic should feel effortless to the caller. Even if your agent is performing dozens of operations behind the scenes—checking databases, verifying conditions, triggering automations—the user should experience a smooth, conversational flow. The agent sets expectations, explains each step as needed, and reassures callers along the way. A well-designed multi-step flow hides its complexity. Callers feel like the agent is simply "helping them," unaware of the sophisticated logic powering the interaction. This is the hallmark of a professional-grade voice AI agent.

"The Agent Who Could Solve Anything"

Rafael ran a busy plumbing company in a city where emergencies could happen at any hour—burst pipes, leaking heaters, clogged drains, flooded kitchens. His phone rang constantly with panicked customers who needed immediate help. His receptionist did her best, but handling emergencies required quick thinking and multi-step decision-making. She had to identify the urgency, confirm the address, check technician availability, calculate travel times, and schedule the right team. When Rafael began building his AI voice agent "River," he knew the true challenge wasn't answering calls—it was teaching River how to think.

He started by listening to real emergency calls. Every caller had a different way of explaining the same problem. Some shouted. Some whispered. Some rambled for minutes. He noticed something else: every call followed an invisible sequence. First came the panic. Then the explanation. Then the location. Then the request for help. And finally, the relief after a solution was provided. Rafael mapped these stages into Voiceflow: identify emergency → clarify issue → check technician availability → estimate arrival → confirm dispatch. Each stage became a multi-step logic block, and slowly the flow began to resemble the mental checklist his receptionist followed every day.

The first time Rafael tested the multi-step logic, he pretended to be a frantic homeowner. “Uh... my bathroom is flooding—I don’t know what happened—please help,” he said quickly. River responded calmly: “I can help with that. First, what part of your home is affected?” Rafael answered chaotically, but River guided him step by step. After gathering details, River checked technician availability using a connected Google Sheet. When the first technician was booked, River automatically branched into a fallback schedule. When Rafael gave an unclear address, River gently asked for clarification. The agent handled every curveball without hesitation.

But the defining moment came during a real emergency call. A woman named Teresa called late at night, terrified because her basement was filling with water. River immediately detected the urgency based on her tone and words. It moved her into the high-priority route, collected her address, checked available technicians, sent an automated SMS with instructions to prevent further damage, and dispatched the nearest crew. By the time Rafael saw the call log, the situation was already under control. Teresa later said, “Your assistant knew exactly what to do. She saved my basement." That night, Rafael realized River wasn't just following a script—it was making decisions. Smart decisions. Human decisions. The same decisions his receptionist once made, but faster and without error. He listened to the call recording, amazed at how River calmly said, "I'm sending help now. Here's what you should do while we're on the way." Her tone, powered by ElevenLabs, was steady. Her logic, built in Voiceflow, was flawless. Her response time was instant. Rafael sat back in his chair smiling. He had created a problem-solving machine.

And to help others do the same, he shared the exact prompt he used when designing River's multi-step reasoning flows. It became his favorite template—one he wished he'd had when he started:

"Act as a professional no-code voice agent builder. Create a multi-step logic sequence for an emergency service call. Include: clarifying questions, conditional branches for high vs. low urgency, fallback prompts, and variables for address, issue type, and availability. Format it in a way I can copy into Voiceflow."

Anyone who used that prompt, he said, could jumpstart a smart, decision-making voice agent instantly.

Months later, River had become legendary among customers. People trusted her. People relied on her. People admired her. Rafael often heard clients say, "Your assistant saved us," and he smiled every time. River didn't just talk—she solved problems. She thought clearly in chaos. She turned emergencies into order.

Because once she learned multi-step logic, River became unstoppable.

Chapter 9

Adding Memory, Variables, and Dynamic Responses

Memory is one of the most powerful upgrades you can add to a voice AI agent. Without memory, your agent will treat every message in isolation, forcing callers to repeat details and creating robotic, disconnected conversations. With memory, your agent becomes intelligent: it listens, stores information, applies it later in the conversation, and adapts responses dynamically based on what the caller has already said. This transforms the experience from transactional to personal. In Voiceflow, memory is enabled through variables. Variables allow your agent to store details like the caller's name, appointment preferences, account type, problem description, choice selections, and even past responses. When the agent can remember, personalize, and reference previous details, callers feel understood—and trust deepens instantly.

To begin, identify what information your agent should store. This is not about capturing everything at once, but capturing meaningful details that enhance the conversation. Common examples include names, service types, dates, locations, and answers to key questions. In Voiceflow, each piece of data becomes a variable. For example, a variable called {user_name} might hold the caller's name once captured. A variable like {issue_type} could hold the description of the problem. With these variables in place, your agent can say things like "Thanks, John. I'll look into your billing issue now," making the experience feel tailored and human.

Next, consider dynamic responses. A dynamic response changes based on the values stored in variables. Instead of using one generic line, your agent can deliver personalized lines such as: "Since you're calling about your appointment on Tuesday, let me check the availability." Variables make every interaction feel adaptive. Dynamic responses can also adjust tone or flow based on circumstances. For example, if a caller indicates urgency, your agent can switch into an emergency flow. If a caller selects a specific service category, the agent can summarize their choice and follow up with more relevant questions. This ability to adapt gives your agent true conversational intelligence.

An advanced technique is conditional memory. This is when the agent checks whether a variable has already been captured. For example, if {user_name} is empty, the agent asks for it. If not, it skips straight ahead. This prevents repetitive questions. Similarly, if {user_issue} was already stored, the agent can summarize: "You mentioned your water heater is leaking. I'll help you with that." Conditional memory ensures your agent behaves like a real receptionist who listens carefully and doesn't repeat unnecessary steps. It also creates smoother conversations and faster outcomes.

Another powerful concept is long-term memory. While Voiceflow primarily uses session-based memory, you can extend memory through databases, Google Sheets, or CRMs. This allows your agent to recall information from past calls: previous orders, preferred appointment times, loyalty status, recurring issues, or personal preferences. Long-term memory transforms your voice agent from a helpful assistant into a true virtual account manager. With integrations, your agent can automatically fetch data and respond intelligently. This level of personalization dramatically increases user satisfaction and creates a sense of continuity that typical phone systems cannot match.

Finally, you must test memory flows thoroughly. Interrupt yourself mid-sentence. Provide information out of order. Change your mind halfway through. Your agent should store, update, and respond correctly regardless of the order or speed of the conversation. Memory-based systems require careful refinement, but once perfected, they elevate the entire experience. A well-trained memory system makes the difference between "a voice bot" and "an assistant people genuinely love." When an agent remembers, it feels human.

When it remembers correctly, it feels intelligent. And when it uses memory to adapt dynamically, it becomes unforgettable.

"The Assistant Who Never Forgot a Thing"

Priya owned a home cleaning service, and her clients expected personalized attention every time. Some needed weekly deep cleans. Others needed last-minute visits. Some had pets. Some needed eco-friendly products. Some preferred mornings. Others preferred evenings. Remembering small details was essential, but as her business grew, keeping track of everything became overwhelming. When she decided to build her AI voice agent, "Lumi," she had one mission: Lumi had to remember. If Lumi could recall preferences, conditions, schedules, and little details about each client, the service would feel as personal as Priya's own touch.

She spent days mapping out the variables Lumi would need: {client_name}, {cleaning_type}, {frequency}, {pet_present}, {special_notes}, and {preferred_time}. These weren't just technical fields—they were extensions of what her clients cared about most. After integrating these variables into Voiceflow, she tested the system. "Hi, I'm Sarah," she said into the phone. Lumi stored the name. "I need a deep clean, and I have two dogs." Lumi stored the cleaning type and pet details. "Evenings are better for me." Lumi noted the preference. When Lumi responded with, "Thanks, Sarah. I'll make sure our team brings pet-safe supplies and schedules you for an evening slot," Priya felt chills.

The real magic happened during a live call the following week. An older client named Mr. Williamson called sounding forgetful and apologetic. "I... I need cleaning again, but I can't recall what I scheduled last time." Lumi replied gently: "Last time you chose a standard cleaning with eco-friendly products, and you preferred mornings. Would you like the same today?" Mr. Williamson gasped softly. "Yes... yes, that's right. Thank you." His voice cracked with relief. He trusted Lumi immediately. It wasn't just that Lumi remembered—it was that Lumi cared enough to remember.

Word spread quickly. Clients marveled at the "assistant who knows us so well." One customer even joked, "Lumi remembers more about my house than I do." Priya listened to the call recordings, amazed at how naturally Lumi adapted. When a client changed their mind mid-call, Lumi updated the variables seamlessly. When someone mentioned a new detail, Lumi referenced it correctly minutes later. When a client returned weeks later, Lumi recalled the most recent service. Priya realized she hadn't just built efficiency—she had built loyalty.

And because Priya wanted other business owners to

experience the same transformation, she created a prompt that anyone could use. It became one of her go-to templates—simple, powerful, and immediately useful:

"Act as a professional no-code voice agent designer. Create a memory-based conversation flow with variables for name, service type, preferences, and special notes. Include dynamic responses that reference these variables and conditional checks that prevent repeated questions. Format it so I can copy it into Voiceflow."

Every entrepreneur she shared it with saw immediate improvements. Lumi became famous in her community. Customers listened to her warm, familiar voice and felt cared for. They trusted her. They relied on her. And Priya smiled every time someone said, "Your assistant never forgets a thing."

Because Lumi didn't just store data. She remembered people.

Chapter 10

Handling Interruptions, Overlaps, and Natural Speech Patterns

Human conversations rarely follow perfect, linear patterns. People interrupt. They talk over the agent. They change their minds mid-sentence. They pause for long stretches. They speak quickly, slowly, emotionally, or unclearly. A truly human-like voice agent must navigate this natural chaos with grace. Handling interruptions and natural speech patterns is one of the most advanced—and necessary—skills your agent must master. Without this, callers will feel like they're talking to a rigid machine. With it, your agent will feel alive, flexible, and capable of responding like a real human working at a front desk.

The first step is enabling barge-in behavior. Barge-in allows callers to interrupt your agent while it is speaking. Humans interrupt constantly when they understand what's being asked or when they feel urgency. Voiceflow and many telephony systems support barge-in, allowing your agent to stop mid-sentence the moment the caller begins speaking. This creates a smoother interaction and prevents frustration. Without barge-in, callers must wait for the agent to finish every line, which feels slow and robotic. With barge-in enabled, conversations flow naturally because callers feel in control. Next, the agent must handle unclear or partial speech. People often speak in fragments: "Yeah uh... Tuesday... actually wait... maybe Wednesday?" A well-trained agent must detect hesitation, uncertainty, or corrections. This is where layered prompts come in. Instead of relying on one rigid question, you build flexible prompts and follow-ups. For example: "What day works best for you? You can say Tuesday, Wednesday, or another date." This gives callers multiple natural patterns to latch onto. When callers give incomplete answers, fallback prompts guide them gently without sounding repetitive.

Pauses are another important factor. Some callers need time to think. Others become emotional or confused. Your agent must recognize silence not as failure but as space. Intelligent agents respond after thoughtful delays or offer supportive phrases like: "Take your time—I'm listening," or "No rush, whenever you're ready." This builds emotional trust and prevents the caller from feeling pressured. Voiceflow allows you to configure no-input timers so your agent reacts to silence with empathy rather than generic confusion.

Another advanced feature is real-time corrections. Callers frequently change their answers mid-process. For example, "Book it for Friday. No actually—Saturday." Your agent must override the previous variable and update the conversation flow without breaking. This requires careful logic and dynamic variable handling. When implemented correctly, the agent feels truly human—capable of adjusting and adapting instantly. It also reduces caller frustration because they don't need to restart entire processes just to correct one detail.

Accents, speed variations, and emotional tones must also be considered. Some callers speak quickly. Others speak slowly. Some slur words from stress or fatigue. Through robust STT (speech-to-text) and diverse training utterances, your agent becomes capable of handling a wide range of real-world voices. Testing with different speakers—young, old, native English speakers, non-native speakers—helps ensure your agent performs consistently across demographics. The goal is inclusivity: an agent that understands everyone equally.

Finally, interruptions and natural speech patterns must be supported by thoughtful script design. Agents should avoid long monologues. Instead, use short phrases, natural pacing, and optional clarifications. The smoother and more flexible your conversation design becomes, the more callers will feel like your agent truly "gets them." When an AI handles real-world speech gracefully, it creates a moment of magic—callers forget they're talking to a machine. Mastering interruptions, overlaps, and natural speech patterns is the final step in creating a voice agent that feels genuinely alive. With this skill, your agent becomes more than a digital helper—it becomes a believable conversational partner capable of handling real human communication.

"The Assistant Who Could Keep Up With Anyone"

Carlos ran a busy HVAC company, and if there was one thing he understood, it was chaotic phone calls. Most customers called when something urgent was happening—the AC died in the heat, the heater broke in winter, or a unit was making a loud, frightening noise. People spoke fast, talked over the receptionist, rambled, panicked, repeated themselves, and changed their answers mid-sentence. When Carlos built his AI voice agent "Nora," he knew she had to handle real conversations, not perfect ones. Nora had to be able to keep up with anyone.

He started by observing how people behaved on the phone. Customers interrupted constantly, especially when they were stressed. They rarely waited for a question to finish. They often answered before the receptionist was done speaking. Carlos added barge-in features so Nora would stop talking the moment a caller spoke. The first time he tested it, he interrupted her mid-sentence: "Hi this is Nora fro—" "Yeah my heater broke." Nora immediately pivoted: "I can help with that. When did the issue start?" Carlos laughed out loud. It felt exactly like watching a human adjust mid-conversation.

The next challenge was handling mid-sentence corrections. During real calls, customers would say things like, "It's been broken since Friday—no wait, Thursday night." Nora needed to gracefully update the information. Using conditional variables and override logic, Carlos taught her to confirm updates naturally. When he tested it, she said, "Got it—Thursday night. I'll use that." It was simple, but it felt human. It felt right. Clients wouldn't feel judged. They'd feel understood.

Nora's biggest test came on a scorching summer afternoon when a frantic caller dialed in shouting over the noise of a failing AC unit. He spoke fast, emotional, and barely coherent: "It's making this horrible sound and my kids are overheating I need someone RIGHT NOW—wait—actually—can someone come tonight?" Nora handled his rapid speech, interruptions, and emotional tone with remarkable calm. "I'll help you right away. First, tell me your address so we can dispatch a technician." When he paused in panic, she reassured him: "Take your time—I'm here." She waited patiently, then guided him step by step. By the end of the call, the man said softly, "Thank you. I can breathe now."

Carlos listened to the recording later that night and felt a lump in his throat. Nora didn't just provide information—she handled chaos with grace. She adapted to the caller's interruptions, updated details on the fly, responded to emotions, and guided him with stability. It was exactly how he wanted his business to treat people in distress. She had become the assistant who could keep up with anyone—fast talkers, nervous callers, emotional parents, elderly customers—everyone.

Inspired by how powerful this transformation was, Carlos wrote down the exact prompt he used to train Nora's interruption-handling logic so others could adopt the same approach. He shared it with fellow contractors who wanted their own agents to feel human:

"Act as a no-code voice agent expert. Create a conversation flow that supports barge-in interruption handling, real-time corrections, hesitation detection, and dynamic variable updates. Include natural fallback prompts like 'Take your time' or 'No problem, let's adjust that.' Format the output so I can paste it into Voiceflow."

When others tried it, they immediately saw their agents change—becoming smoother, more adaptive, more human-like. Nora continued taking hundreds of calls every week, always ready, always calm, always keeping up.

She never missed a beat, no matter how chaotic the caller was.

Chapter 11

Twenty Powerful Prompts to Practice Voice AI Agent Building

How to Use These Prompts and Where to Enter Them

Before reviewing the prompts, you must understand **how and where** to use them. All the prompts in this chapter are designed to be pasted into:

1. ChatGPT (GPT-4 / GPT-5 / GPT-4o or higher) Use it to generate:

- Conversation scripts
- Voiceflow flow templates
- Multi-step logic sequences
- Memory variables
- Intent utterances
- Dynamic response templates
- Error handling flows
- Sample dialogues

- Voice personality profiles
- Optimization checklists

2. Claude, Gemini, or any advanced LLM As long as the model supports structured output, it will work.

3. Voiceflow AI Step / OpenAI API Fields Some prompts can be placed directly inside:

- **AI blocks**
- **Assistant tasks**
- **Knowledge injection prompts**
- **Intent training fields**

Whenever a prompt says "Format this for Voiceflow," the model will output:

- Blocks
- Variables
- Branches
- Speak prompts
- Capture prompts

- Conditions
- Integrations

These make it easy for you to **copy and paste directly into Voiceflow**, saving hours of manual design.

THE 20 PROMPTS

Each includes an explanation of what it does, how to use it, and where to paste it.

1. The Universal Voice Agent Starter Prompt

Prompt: *"Act as a professional no-code voice agent architect. Create a complete call flow for my industry, including intents, variables, fallback prompts, and sample dialogues. Format the output for Voiceflow."*

Use: To generate a full starting blueprint for any business.
Where to paste: ChatGPT → copy result → paste into Voiceflow canvas.

2. The Voice Personality Builder Prompt

Prompt: *"Create a voice personality profile including tone, phrasing style, emotional attributes, pacing, and vocabulary. Write Speak block examples that match this personality."*

Use: To define exactly how the AI should speak. **Where:** ChatGPT first → then paste lines into Voiceflow Speak blocks.

3. The ElevenLabs Script Optimization Prompt

Prompt: *"Rewrite my script to sound natural when spoken aloud by ElevenLabs. Add natural pauses, shorten sentences, and increase warmth."*

Use: To make scripts sound human. **Where:** ChatGPT → then paste results into Voiceflow.

4. The Multi-Step Logic Flow Creator Prompt

Prompt: *"Create a multi-step decision tree for this task, including conditions, branches, and variables. Format for Voiceflow."*

Use: For building advanced flows. **Where:** ChatGPT → Voiceflow logic blocks.

5. The Intent Training Prompt

Prompt: *"Generate 30 utterances for each of these intents. Include variations across tone, slang, accents, and fragmented speech."*

Use: To train the intent engine robustly. **Where:** Voiceflow → Intent block → paste utterances.

6. The Memory Variable Blueprint Prompt

Prompt: *"Create a list of conversational variables my agent should store for personalization. Include examples of dynamic responses for each variable."*

Use: For building personalization. **Where:** ChatGPT → then into variable list in Voiceflow.

7. The Error & Fallback Enhancer Prompt

Prompt: *"Rewrite my fallback prompts to feel warm, patient, and natural. Include three variations for misunderstandings and silence."*

Use: Improve clarity and comfort during errors. **Where:** ChatGPT → Voiceflow fallback prompts.

8. The Interruption/Barge-In Training Prompt

Prompt: *"Create interruption-friendly phrasing and short Speak prompts optimized for barge-in behavior."*

Use: Makes the agent resilient to interruptions. **Where:** ChatGPT → Voiceflow Speak blocks.

9. The Real Conversation Simulator Prompt

Prompt: *"Simulate a real caller with emotional tone,*

interruptions, fast speech, and corrections. Test my script and show where improvements are needed."

Use: To stress-test the flow. **Where:** ChatGPT only.

10. The Complex Task Generator Prompt

Prompt: *"Build a multi-step flow for scheduling, rescheduling, and canceling appointments. Include all logic branches and variables."*

Use: When building appointment-heavy agents. **Where:** ChatGPT → Voiceflow canvas.

11. The CRM Integration Flow Prompt

Prompt: *"Create formatted API request templates for updating a CRM with user data. Include variables and JSON examples."*

Use: For Make.com, Zapier, or API integration. **Where:** ChatGPT → Voiceflow → HTTP blocks.

12. The Tone Switching Prompt

Prompt: *"Create responses for three tones—normal, empathetic, urgent—triggered by caller keywords or emotion."*

Use: For emotional intelligence. **Where:** ChatGPT → Voiceflow conditions.

13. The Data Collection Optimizer Prompt

Prompt: *"Rewrite my data collection questions to be short, clear, and interruption-friendly."*

Use: Improves capture accuracy. **Where:** ChatGPT → Voiceflow Capture blocks.

14. The Industry-Specific Vocabulary Prompt

Prompt: *"Generate a vocabulary list and intent utterances specific to my industry. Include synonyms and slang."*

Use: Makes the agent smarter in niche fields. **Where:** Voiceflow → Intent blocks.

15. The Scenario Stress-Test Prompt

Prompt: *"Throw unpredictable callers at my agent. Include angry callers, confused callers, quiet callers, and rushed callers. Show how my agent should respond."*

Use: Reveals weak points. **Where:** ChatGPT.

16. The Rapid Flow Prototyping Prompt

Prompt: *"Create a one-minute rapid prototype version of* *my flow with condensed steps."*

Use: Fast iteration. **Where:** ChatGPT then Voiceflow.

17. The Voice Behavior Enhancer Prompt

Prompt: *"Optimize my script for pacing, warmth, clarity, and human-like delivery using ElevenLabs settings."*

Use: Enhances realism. **Where:** ChatGPT → then into Voiceflow.

18. The Caller Memory Recall Prompt

Prompt: *"Create recall statements my agent can use when repeating stored information, such as name, preferences, or last service."*

Use: Adds personalization. **Where:** Voiceflow dynamic responses.

19. The Database Query Prompt

Prompt: *"Create a structured flow for checking availability from a database or Google Sheet. Include errors, timeouts, and fallback branches."*

Use: For any data lookup. **Where:** Voiceflow → integrations.

20. The Final Agent Polishing Prompt

Prompt: *"Evaluate my entire script and identify 10 improvements to make it sound more natural, supportive, and human."*

Use: Final refinement before going live. **Where:** ChatGPT.

Epilogue

The Future Speaks Through Your Voice Agents

As you reach the end of this book, one truth becomes unmistakably clear: the world is moving toward voice-first automation faster than most people realize. Businesses that embrace this transformation today will operate with advantages that were once unimaginable—unlimited call-handling capacity, zero missed opportunities, instant responsiveness, and emotionally intelligent assistants available every hour of the day. You now understand the foundations: designing natural conversations, training intent, deploying memory, integrating ElevenLabs, connecting telephony, building multi-step logic, handling interruptions, and personalizing the entire experience. You have the tools. You have the templates. You have the prompts. And most importantly, you have the mindset required to build something extraordinary.

But the real magic begins now—when you take what you've learned and start building voice agents tailored to your world, your customers, your needs, and your vision. The greatest breakthroughs will not come from copying what others create, but from inventing solutions that solve problems uniquely relevant to your own business. Whether you build an AI receptionist for your clinic, an intake agent for your law office, an emergency triage assistant, a customer support system, a lead qualification agent, or even a voice-based personal assistant for your daily life, you now have the framework needed to make it real. And every agent you build will sharpen your skills and expand your imagination.

The rise of voice automation is not about replacing people. It is about giving humans more time, more clarity, and more freedom. Voice agents eliminate repetitive tasks so you can focus on creative, strategic, and high-value work. They standardize quality so customers always receive exceptional service. They capture details with precision. They reduce friction. They simplify workflows. They act with perfect consistency. They empower small businesses to operate with the sophistication of enterprise-level organizations—without requiring enterprise-level staffing or budgets. And for entrepreneurs, creators, and innovators, voice agents unlock entirely new business models, revenue streams, and opportunities.

As you move forward, remember that the voice agent you build is a reflection of your values. Your agent's tone communicates your brand personality. Its logic expresses your level of care. Its memory demonstrates your commitment to personalization. Its patience reflects your empathy. When callers interact with your voice agent, they are interacting with a piece of you—your vision, your design, your standards, and your ambition. Treat your agent as a true team member. Improve it. Refine it. Coach it. Expand it. The more attention you give, the more powerful it becomes.

The future belongs to those who automate intelligently. You now stand at the frontier of a revolution that will reshape how businesses operate and how people communicate with technology. While others wait for AI to define their future, you are building it—conversation by conversation, logic block by logic block, and prompt by prompt. The voice agents you create will not only elevate your systems—they will elevate your customers' experiences, your brand reputation, and your competitive advantage. And as the technology continues to evolve, your skills will naturally evolve with it, placing you among the leaders of the no-code AI movement.

Your journey doesn't end here. This epilogue marks the beginning of your next chapter. The world needs creators who can build voice agents with clarity, empathy, and intelligence. Your clients need it. Your business needs it. And the future of automation depends on innovators like you—people willing to learn, adapt, and bring new ideas to life. Now, equipped with the knowledge in this book, you have everything required to build voice agents that speak with impact, think with logic, and serve with excellence. The future is speaking. Your job is to give it the right voice.

www.ingramcontent.com/pod-product-compliance
Lightning Source LLC
LaVergne TN
LVHW022016200926
848481LV00007B/2425
* 9 7 9 8 2 9 5 4 5 3 9 0 8 *